I0162925

BLACK GINGER

the book of whiskey

Dave Thompson

thank you to Brittany Rauch for reading it
when she had so many other,
better things to do

thank you to the Wagners for pen in hand
and for helping to scatter me,
thank you to Sera and Julien for dancing,
and thank you to Tony, Doranne, Jason and Kris

to the snake,
the knife
and the stone

forty into three

I could, you know
just burn upon you
a simple scar

one

3.20.09 | Home

It is the addictions I adopt
in a steady
rolling out back-beat,
that remember what remains of my anger
and they remember when
what it meant,
it meant it in my veins
potent and read in a staccato voice
or sung in chorus
around a stoned goat.

4.2.09 | Home

Gotta remember to keep up on my toes
and let myself, finally
just shut up.

I dig for my pulse in my finger.
Is that what I feel?
Or is it a guitar
shattering on in the background
not unsad but,
rhythmically strumming . . .

Please I say
stay out of the clamoring upon;
it is already a freight-train cock fight.

I'm so, I don't know . . .
look at me:
with warm feet
in the thick of my blur . . .

You know it will happen suddenly,
when you fail to
plan to
keep at least one step outside the line
sweet jesus . . .
I seek that thought that
smears us all across oncoming pavements
in a morning rushhour
uncaffeinated screech

Or perhaps,
some cello . . .

10.9.09 | Home

Count quick!
a sharp one two, one two,
I am the boom
the boom boom master
mister american gothic with
a pitchfork
and a jerry-curl
oh yeah . . . there I find it,
in the kaleidoscope grey thick fire in my head
but, what I can be amazed at
easily betrays me.

When we all seem to float
in quick
suspended unison,
beware!
For I am a wiccan delirious
semi-high priestess
and I spread deeply within you.

If, I could reach it everyday
the slippery stream
and the shimmering groove
of my secret smoking blues . . .

I send prayers for "fuck,
what a way this is to begin . . ."

I ask myself,
why do I appear so contained?
I need to believe in me
but my vampire, my staccato
and my growl,
they look for something to destroy.

8.9.10 | Black Mountain

When the world becomes dust
and soaks into my lungs,
we will breed our young
to feed our young
and die before they age.

I want to live where the grass lows into the wind,
girls still ride horses,
my spirit is a blister
and my ideas a greasy hot
pork-chop
dragged across your face.

I once walked through a god
through a shadow that flew from a tree.

12.25.10 | Home

When life itself is a weapon,
arm yourself.
Swing your chin and swing your chi
and let's all keep your pieces together.

These pants make you taller
and make me hard.

My heart is odd-shaped,
it has my blood in it.

I am nothing, it seems
but self-referential these days,
especially when angrily listening to bauhaus
late on christmas evening.

I walk with my knife in my teeth,
almost satisfied
with your juices; red, wild and subjugated
slowly drying in my beard.

You forget yourself and continue
to breath into me
long after I have.

12.31.10 | Black Mountain

My wife makes me walk
when rather I'd hum,
and she sleeps while I dream
of making it right
or at least, better.

But all I have
is this misspelled dream
out of focus,
in strokes of hallucinogenic perfection.

3.12.11 | Black Mountain

Under a flock of origami cranes,
I fall into moments when I do not think of you
and my ears ring in arrhythmia to the overhead chorus,
while a machete lays
foolishly across my legs
vibrating with danger
and contemplating my serrated iron flesh.

5.28.11 | Black Mountain

My urgent miss madame soleil,
across your face: ashes,
and cactus flowers and distortion
flowing from your slightly parted legs
showing me
how strongly
you commit to a dangerous future.

10.1.11 | Black Mountain

Killer, in plural
I give away my swagger and
I think I may take to the heroin
were you to knock me out and die.

Baby, oh baby
I do so dream of wolves;
thirsty,
drooling,
fucking, human wolves
and getting finally hard,
the ravenous hunger deepens me.

The lengths of our lives are alone and ungathered
we are,
in-fucking-credible
as a half-crescent moon
coming alive,
on a dead-end firefly road.

10.27.11 | Black Mountain

I want to die like darkness
clarified into night.
The warmth hammers against my left,
the cold against my right.

The pen is the axe of the devil
and the cock of the mad dog.

2.13.12 | Black Mountain

It ain't dark enough yet, my love
to not stop dying yet, my love
when choking upon the moment
your blood dissolved to dust.

I want to say . . .
. . . it was summer
and deep grooves beneath the swing, my love
declared my life to the world.

In fits of drifting anger,
I leave you very slowly.
Almost forty years along, my love
almost forty years along

3.17.12 | Home

Were it not for you, my love
I may have never,
suddenly
understood abandonment.

It's as if my life began again;
the second of many
forgettings of everything
at the age of five, scared and
too frail and sturdy, my love
to carry you too.

4.17.12 | Home

Before I was
there is, I remember
a picture of a boy and
a decent man in the snow.

In my dreams, it is dark
and a woman laughed at the door
as yet unlost to everyone,
and still my mother.

That's as far as I ever get.
That's as far as I ever go.

I put my life in motion before
I was shown the path to take

what hits me
hits me with the sad fate
of hitting me hard

two

1.5.13 | Home

The sickness, I confess
it rattles within me
a sick, sweet electric sickness
in my fingers, in my face, in my balls
and in the ring out of focus
to my high old eyes.

No one loves this me,
but what love would I
for what I would become,
seeking not the sickness that rattles within me
but instead,
the sickness I rattle within?

Bears wander this life,
rarely afraid.

Finally in bed
alone save for this machete,
I pause,
when I have to.

1.12.13 | Home

The life in my throat;
quiet, atrophied, sinewed
flickers its strength
through half closed eyes
yet, so clearly in focus;
the dream of acres of gravestones
winter-dark and sexy, yeah . . .

If only life was louder tonight:
the music and the breathing,
the pen and the sex
if only it was louder and
not dreamt within a crow,
but inhaled by the wolf.

It is hard
but not impossible,
to see everything there is in the dark.

1.25.13 | Home

What happened to my hard cock
in the grips of death
and an icy dark wind
violent and once permahard
and available to almost no one?

My grandfather would be proud
not at my size;
but for the anger and the whiskey way
with which I whip it around,
with which I whip it around.

Maybe it is what I crave;
the fight against myself,
wolf against moose,
moose against wolf.

2.1.13 | Home

In my dreaming, you are dying,
and I am racing crazily away
at one
with the drive and the certainty of time until
a rogue mongoloid
turns to me and sneers.
I count him to the list of my dead.

In everything it appears, there is death.
In everything there is dust and breath and rust.
Silence is the gift given to us
before we begin to scream,
not at the fear,
but at the truth.

No one knows it and
no one listens
my dystopia cares not for you,
you care not for it.

Chester purrs in the dead dog's bed
not yet released, only ten days dead.
Chester purrs in the dead dogs bed
only now, only ten days dead.

He wants to hear me coming
following the fog he was
light and heavy and
hanging close to the ground,
dark and invisible and impossible to see from within.

2.13.13 | Home

Oh! the fingers around my throat
as every thought
beguiles me at once and
everything goes
just,
silent . . .

. . . save for the melody,
slowly building in my head.

Beware! I say, for I am the Lord your God
and these words,
they are the fucking word of the Lord.
I create and I destroy with
the thinking of the thought and I will love you
until I love you no more.

With but seven breaths of smoke and thought
I cure fire within the earth,
I cum fire into the wombs of
all the beasts and the daughters I breathe within
for I am God and the Word, and the Word is my blood
my life and my lust
Beware! I say, for this is the seed of your Lord.

2.16.13 | Home

When I hear you,
In the distance
I can hear the distance
and the dull, the ghosts
and the growl.

When I listen,
when I hear
I cannot remember who this is.

Somewhere there is a door
and outside, there is me.

2.20.13 | Home

The whiskey you give me
It scatters me
and my mouth is filled with orchids.

3.9.13 | Black Mountain

My feet must be bare
and writhing against skin
or wood
or stone or snow
one foot deep and covered in stars.

All my faults and my sick bald head,
they are always forgiven
when I am able to lay my bare balls upon the earth.

My lord,
this burst red river
how it rings in my ears
while the smoke and the wind
drizzle down my throat;
a lost art and
a demon
strummed at the top of the mountain.

3.14.13 | Home

I will line my walls with you,
knots and faults and
one-closed-eye orgasms,
pushed by the wind
and the grain of my tongue
into a danger
I lick off my fingers.

A softness on my left,
and a knife on my right,
I wear you through to both sides.

3.27.13 | Home

Oh lord, I hear
the beating of your hammer.

It believed itself to be
a reverberating heart
stone, steel and
the earth my blood drips upon.

The lost skin of your neck
and the rhythms of your face, they
turn away and
your black jungle ginger
of sinews and a single
chameleon dark eye,
they do not attempt to hide from me.

My feet are wine and wild.
My feet are wine.
My feet are wild.

Oh, this life in my hands
mutant child come to me
surely when you are dead
I will love you.
Oh mutant child, come to me.

4.5.13 | Black Mountain

Eventually,
I may control the growl
but, until then . . .

I am a hurtling instrument of death,
I am a hurtling instrument of life,
I am playing with death and thinking with fire
I am playing with death, I am thinking with fire.

Oh dear woman
touch yourself and think of how I touch you
and you do not touch me.

In the dark the sharpness
feels like the absence of everything but it,
and in the dark,
I feel like you and you feel like vibrating.

If this doesn't get me there
nothing will

three

4.26.13 | Home

To awake, slit and dead
and no longer dying . . .

Sometimes I feel the need,
sometimes I feel the knife
and when I float right through them
each, we are the same.

Quickly I breathe
and the disconnect begins
between was and then.

4.29.13 | Home

When I make you cry
and I've made you cry . . .

5.4.13 | Home

Even the shoelace, untied side down
in my boot is a frown
judging my frailty
with an axe behind its back.

My flank flinches at your touch
and my arms feel strange around you,
stretched out and dreaming
of the unthinkable.

5.9.13 | Home

The claw dreams of dreaming
seeking to destroy
just enough to keep living.

5.17.13 | Home

I cup you, spirit in my hand
the cure I seek;
stone, and cornered within my fingers.

A knife, a snake and a sneer;
you fit within my fist
and one-eyed, you appear.

I see your smile only when
you are half buried
and breathing wildly
"at last . . ."

5.28.13 | Black Mountain

The world
is just what I believe it to be;
it's always me
and the whiskey
a wife,
and a rumbling I barely hear, but
always feel.

And the nudity
always the nudity;
the black ginger sage I breathe out
in loose bare foot air.

5.29.13 | Black Mountain

What is, is just what there is
wherever you are,
and the faces in the pebbles in the dirt
are just faces in the pebbles in the dirt;
one of them is a skull,
and none of them vibrate at all.

What lives, lives only because
it has not yet died.
The cactus and the free man
all live until they die
and we will,
and we do.

5.31.13 | Black Mountain

Now that it is coming from two sides,
it feels like all sides and
a rabbit hole of sand.

We are seeming suddenly
not as 3-D, as we
have always believed outselves to be;
to be swallowed from all sides
by a little distortion.

6.1.13 | Black Mountain

I still hear you pounce
your feet heavy on the ground;
lion upon the earth,
wind when within the trees.

7.5.13 | Black Mountain

It is not just the opium,
the calm night air
and the thump I hear
bounding on the ground
oh dancer, it is
the twisted grin of your mind,
the breath rushing back against mine
the bleed, the confluence
and the surge . . .

7.12.13 | Home

Tonight I will divide
into wild and righteous
bare from adolecence down,
an anger coming at you
lost and full of whisky
and dying to be your song.

But now,
I seek only the wet wood of the storm
against my crisp bare ass,
while I think about
how far out
this darkness extends.

7.20.13 | Home

I am your lord of time and light
for, I know
the moon is still
five days from full.

I promise you
I am never over it.

8.23.13 | Black Mountain

What wait you for, my undone child
the sea sings white
and the dirt churns wild,
what wait you for?
I know I should understand you.
I know I should understand you.
But you speak to me,
it seems
only in our dreams.

9.18.13 | Home

Oh, the knife I was;
never as sharp as I shall want
and never as blunt
as I can be,
sinking the edge into skin
too sharp to be thin
and asleep in my hand, until I catch myself
and abruptly recall
that last night,
I dreamed once more of the hole.

There are too many sharks in this life
and not enough teeth
to dull the blade
infinitely more deadly in my hands
than in my heart,
than in my heart,
than in my sharp, old heart.

Seduced by the blood,
knowing only the meaning,
knowing only the reason,
knowing only almost everything . . .
I walk drunk,
become old
and fuck how I want to fuck;
hard and scared.

About the author

I have known the Author for almost two decades now, and nothing he does has ever ceased to amaze me – yes, be that bad, or good. He is a strange and unique combination of both eccentricity and wholly-grounded well-centeredness, which should, of course, make for some pretty damn great poetry, as long as the majority of the poems contained herein do not center around a certain part of his anatomy that, for some reason, he's always seemed to be overly proud of. All this being said, I ask you now, why are you reading my opinion of him? Open the damn book and see how great he is for yourself!

~ Anthony Michael Punko, esq.

Daves' formative years proved to be challenging . . . for those around him. While in his early to mid teens, he developed several habits that proved to be rather troublesome. His habit of locking his teachers out of their classrooms was not as disturbing as his delight in unzipping the clothing of unsuspecting young females. Dave's vacant good looks and his blond Amish bowl-cut got him out of a lot of trouble in his youth.

Throughout his late teens, Dave discovered a deep appreciation for sleep deprivation, alcohol, ladies knee-highs and his right hand. His "catch phrase" soon became "oh, the chaffing".

– Doranne Menotti

From pink slip to poignant texts, words are his weapon and wand.

– Kristine Molinary

I agree with the other guys on this page; the author can be kind of an asshole. Well... at least the honest contributors. When I first met Dave, I had been warned that that he's the kind of guy that would end up punching you in the gut. I also noticed that the smart people begrudgingly liked him. With Dave, if you put in the time and stick it out you'll end up with the best kind of friend.

Dave is aggressively honest in so many aspects. His wit and reckless regard for your feelings make him endearing. Good or bad, I've never heard him tell a lie. More than once, his comments have sucked the air out of the room leaving behind only gasps. He has never missed a deadline. For all these reasons, you want him on your side.

I have witnessed many of Dave's artistic skills including graphic design, music and carving. His dedication and attention to detail lead me to expect that the book in your hands is worth three reads.

– Jason Dicus